CW01652461

Taming Tessa

written by Jenny Alexander
illustrated by Ken Stott

Chapter One

The Terrible Teens

Ben had always found it quite difficult living with Tessa. He thought she was noisy, messy and bad-tempered. His mum and dad said she would grow out of it. But Tessa just seemed to grow noisier, messier and more bad-tempered every day.

She had always played her music quite loudly, but now she played it very loudly indeed. She had music blaring from her room at all hours of the day and night. If anyone asked her to turn it down, she would shout above the noise,

"Why should I?"

Even when the music wasn't on, Tessa seemed to prefer shouting to talking normally. Then, when she had finished yelling, she liked to flounce out and slam the door. Ben wondered if she had actually forgotten how to close a door quietly.

Tessa's bedroom
had always been untidy,
but now it was so bad that all
her stuff spilled out onto the landing,
and halfway down the stairs. Ben often had
to step over dirty socks, old tissues, bits of cotton
wool and homework in order to get to his own room.

Sometimes a cluster of dirty
coffee mugs appeared on
the landing, like a sudden
growth of mushrooms.
Often, they had a bit of old
grey coffee in the bottom,
with little islands of blue
mould floating on the top.

Tessa didn't only make a mess in her bedroom. She had taken to leaving her things all over the house. She couldn't watch television without leaving the room more littered than a football stadium after a big match.

But if anyone drew attention to it ...

"Tessa, you forgot to tidy up your snack, dear ..." she would just turn round and scream ...

"Why should I?"

Then everyone would brace themselves for the slam of the door and the stamp of her feet on the stairs.

Often, Ben's mum would ask *him* to clear Tessa's things away. It wasn't fair. And as Tessa refused to do anything around the house, or did it very badly, he ended up doing her jobs as well.

But when he asked his mum and dad to do something about Tessa, they just shrugged. Girls of Tessa's age were supposed to be moody, they said. She was going through the Terrible Teens.

"But it isn't fair!" Ben protested. "You don't let me slam doors and yell at everyone."

"Do you want to slam doors and yell at everyone?"

Ben had to admit that he didn't really.

"Let's cross that bridge when we come to it then, shall we?"

They told him to try to be patient. After all, Tessa had been patient with him, when he was going through the Terrible Twos.

Then, he didn't just stamp and shout, slam doors and make a mess – he chewed her school books, dribbled on everything and put her toys in the toilet.

At least Tessa didn't do **that!**

But Ben didn't want to be patient. Being patient just made him feel angry. Sooner or later, something would have to be done about Tessa. If everyone else wanted to turn a blind eye, so be it! Ben would find a way of tackling the problem himself.

Chapter Two

Enough!

It was Monday morning. Ben went to the fridge to get some milk for his cereal. There was only an empty bottle. "Who took all the milk? Did you, Tessa?" he snapped.

"What if I did?" said Tessa. She was cutting some bread for her packed lunch.

Their mother came in. "Could you wash up your bowl please, Tessa?" she asked.

"Why should I?"

yelled Tessa. She tossed the bread into the bin and flounced out, slamming the door behind her.

Ben's mum asked him to clear the table when he had finished, and then she left the room as well. He went to pick up Tessa's bowl. It was full of milk, with one or two Korn Krunchies floating on top. She had taken all the milk – and then left it! He was furious.

"That's it!"

he growled. "I've had enough!"

He left everything on the table and went to school without any breakfast. He didn't feel hungry any more.

"What's wrong with you?" asked Mouse and Jojo, as they all waited at the crossing.

"I'll tell you later," he said. He was too cross to talk about it.

It took until dinner time for Ben to calm down enough to talk to his friends. First, he told them about the milk, but they didn't seem to think that was any big deal. So he told them some of the other things that Tessa did. Mouse wanted to know why Ben's parents weren't making Tessa behave better. Ben told him what they said about the Terrible Teens.

"I don't think my brother Mick's been through the Terrible Teens," remarked Billy.

"Perhaps it's only girls, then," Ravi suggested.

Sam smacked his arm. "Get lost!" she said.

"It looks like Ravi's right," said Mouse, and they all began to laugh.

But Ben wasn't laughing. "What am I going to do?" he said. "Our house is like a war zone. It hasn't been this bad since Fatcat first arrived ..."

They all nodded, remembering what Fatcat was like in her younger days.

She shredded the curtains, she chewed the carpets, and she raided the rubbish bins.

She slept in the saucepans and refused to use her litter tray.

If anyone told her off, she spat and snarled and she bared her teeth. She was a cat with a bad attitude all right.

"Fatcat's okay now, though, isn't she?" said Jojo. "So she must have grown out of it."

"Perhaps your mum and dad are right," agreed Sam.

Ben sighed. "She didn't just grow out of it on her own," he said. "We had to tame her."

Donut looked thoughtful. "If you can tame a cat, then perhaps you can tame a teenager," he said.

"Hmm ..." Ben gave it some thought. It was either a stupid idea or a brainwave. He couldn't quite make up his mind which.

Chapter Three

The Secret of Success

After school, Ben and Fatcat were sprawled on the sofa, sharing a packet of chocolate biscuits. Fatcat was watching television. Ben was watching Fatcat.

Taming Fatcat had been quite straightforward. She had to be rewarded for good behaviour with a tasty titbit, and punished for bad behaviour with a firm telling-off.

Tessa came in with a mug of coffee in one hand and a bowl of peanuts in the other. She picked up the remote and flicked the channels, not bothering to check if Ben minded. Fatcat miaowed at her, crossly.

Ben wasn't interested in the television because he was too busy studying his sister.

She undid her shoes
and kicked them off.

Then she took off her
jumper and dropped
it on the floor.

She sipped her coffee,
slopping it over the
coffee table as she put
the mug down again.

She scattered
peanuts on the rug.

"Hello," said Ben.

Tessa glanced at him, then turned back to watch the television without saying a word.

Ben reckoned Donut's idea was worth a try. He had nothing to lose. If he didn't manage to tame Tessa, he would probably have to kill her. So when she got up and made for the door, leaving all her rubbish behind, he said, "Don't forget your stuff."

Tessa gave him a withering look and walked out.

At least she didn't slam the door.

Ben followed his sister into the kitchen. She was looking for something else to eat. "I've got some chocolate biscuits here," he said. "You can have one if you clear up your stuff in the living room."

Tessa ignored him and went on searching through the cupboards. He thought she was waiting for a better offer. He had some toffees in his pocket. "I'll give you a toffee if you tidy up," he said, holding one out to show her. She looked at him as if he was a beetle and she couldn't decide whether to step on him.

"All right," he said. "A toffee *and* a biscuit. That's my best offer."

Tessa took an apple from the fruit bowl, pushed past her brother and went back into the living room. She shoved Fatcat off the sofa and lay down on it. Offering a reward didn't seem to work. Ben decided he should try giving Tessa a tough talking-to. He turned off the television.

Now Tessa looked at him properly for the first time. "What *is* your problem?" she said, her voice full of irritation.

"*You* are my problem!" Ben said. "You leave your things all over the place, you never tidy anything up, you haven't got a nice word for anyone and … and … you use up all the milk at breakfast time!"

"So?" said Tessa.

Ben thought she needed an even tougher telling-off. "So put your shoes and jumper away! Take your mug out to the kitchen! Pick up all those peanuts you have spilt, and wipe the coffee off the table! Go on!

Do it …

NOW!"

Tessa stood up. She took Ben's hand and put her apple core in it. It felt wet and slimy. "Make me," she said.

Ben heard Tessa laughing as she ran up the stairs. Then he heard something else. Little G, their grandmother, was calling through the letterbox. She must have rung the doorbell, but they had not heard her because they were making so much noise.

"What on *earth* is going on?" she asked, as Ben let her in.

Ben took Little G into the living room. He showed her the mess Tessa had left. Little G shrugged and shook her head.

Ben explained that he had been trying to tame Tessa, like they tamed Fatcat. Offering a reward didn't work, he said, so he had been trying a tough talking-to.

"It looks like teenagers can't be tamed, Little G," Ben sighed.

But Little G didn't seem so sure. "What reward did you offer her?" she asked.

"A chocolate biscuit and a toffee," said Ben. "Fatcat would do anything for sweets and biscuits. Actually ... I would, too!"

Little G smiled, "Ah, well, you see – that's where you've been going wrong. Sweets and biscuits work for Fatcat because she loves her food so much. So do you. But Tessa isn't really bothered about food."

"What can we do then?" said Ben.

"Find out what Tessa really likes. When it comes to rewards, that is the secret of success."

Chapter Four

Taming Tessa

It was easier said than done, finding out what Tessa really liked. Most of the things Ben thought of, she found either boring or stupid. Then, one day when he wasn't even thinking about it, he found out by accident. It happened like this.

Ben had been to Billy's house for tea. He was telling his dad about it, when Tessa suddenly butted in. "Did you see Mick?" she asked.

"Of course I did. He lives there. Anyway ..." Ben turned back to his dad.

But Tessa interrupted again. "Did Mick say anything?"

Ben pointed out that they had all had tea together, so it would have been a bit odd if Mick hadn't said anything at all.

"But did he say anything ... about *me*?" Tessa blurted out. She looked embarrassed.

"I think Tessa likes Mick!" their father remarked. Then Ben knew what to do.

He waited until later, when he and Tessa were alone. "We didn't talk about you today," he said, "but I'll talk about you next time I see Mick."

"What will you say?" asked Tessa.

"I'll tell him you're noisy, messy and untidy, and you leave dirty cups and socks all over the house. I'll tell him if anyone asks you to tidy up, you snap their heads off."

"I'm not *that* bad!" protested Tessa.

Ben didn't need to say anything. He just gave her time to notice the socks stuffed down the side of the sofa, the shoes thrown across the rug, the teacup standing in its dried-up puddle, and the banana skin hanging over the edge of the coffee table.

"You don't *have* to tell him," pleaded Tessa.

Ben pointed out that he saw Mick nearly every day. He could talk about Tessa every time, if she wanted. But being a very honest person, he could only tell the truth. Then Tessa did something very surprising.

She picked up the cup and the banana skin, the socks and shoes, and she took them away.

A few moments later, she came back with a cloth and wiped the table.

That night, Tessa's music wasn't as loud as usual. In fact, it was quite quiet. All the bits of cotton wool and tissues that usually spilled out of her bedroom onto the landing had been cleared away. Ben decided he must make sure he saw Mick the next day.

Mick was helping in the library after school. Ben told him Tessa liked him. Mick looked pleased. He blushed as red as a beetroot. It was clear to Ben that Mick liked Tessa, too.

When Ben got home, Tessa was waiting for him by the front door. "Did you see Mick?" she asked. "What did you say?"

"I said you like him, and you're really nice."

"You told him I like him? Oh, no!"

She covered her face with her hands, but she was obviously glad he had done it. "What did Mick say?"

"He said he likes you, too."

She ran through into the living room and threw herself joyously down on the sofa. Fatcat only just got out of the way in time. "He likes me," she kept saying. "He likes me!"

Ben stood in the doorway, looking at the mugs and crumbs, and the upturned school bag with the books spilling out.

Tessa suddenly sat up and snapped out of it. "Are you going to see him tomorrow?" she asked.

"I could," he replied.

"Can you tell him ..." She thought about it for a few minutes. "Can you tell him I'll be in the park tomorrow, at seven o'clock?"

Ben sat down in the armchair. "All right," he said. "And can you tidy up this mess?"

Tessa jumped up.

"Of course!"